The Endearing Fart

The Endearing Fart

Sad be the ass that can't rejoice

Ilene Dover

Fartologist

TATE PUBLISHING
AND ENTERPRISES, LLC

Published by Tate Publishing & Enterprises, LLC
127 E. Trade Center Terrace | Mustang, Oklahoma 73064 USA
1.888.361.9473 | www.tatepublishing.com

Tate Publishing is committed to excellence in the publishing industry. The company reflects the philosophy established by the founders, based on Psalm 68:11,
"The Lord gave the word and great was the company of those who published it."

Published in the United States of America

ISBN: 978-1-63268-026-6
1. Humor / General
2. Humor / Form / Anecdotes & Quotations
14.03.06

Dedication

Dedicated to the Queen of Farts—that'd be me, thanks to the gene pool of my mother. I'd be happy to share the title with whomever out there is willing.

To my grandson, Herbie, only six, but a little expert on the subject.

To those who contributed their stories.

Contents

Introduction

Has anything ever provided such embarrassment, or even, can we say, pleasure, and well, yes, humor, as the endearing fart? This ethereal "thing" that can make us feel so good yet so ashamed at the same time deserves some special attention and appreciation, don't you think? Whatever else has been so universally common but ignored, experienced, but hidden, loved privately but shunned publicly?

I always believed that if the Queen did it, then we should be able to talk about it even though it may be a bit delicate for those of high distinction such as myself.

Recently, I have had a bout of excessive tooting, which, although not that unusual, led to the thought of sharing the experience. After all, it is my favorite indoor sport, if you know what I mean.

Although the passing of gas is a natural and unstoppable event, it still succeeds in being offensive. If one little bubble squeaks out by mistake, people can be insulted as if you were expressing an opinion even though its intent was obviously not meant to be personal. My, how our conversations would so take on a whole new complexion if we could express our distain in such a way. "Oh really? You know what I think about that! (Cheek lift)...phft...!"

This awkward little book is a result of my being inspired to share with you not only raw moments of my own but also debilitating experiences of others. Yes, I've discovered others too have had excruciatingly embarrassing episodes brought about by the uncontrollable surprise outbreaks of irrepressible "poe-poe" wind.

Therefore, having been in like circumstances yourself, I believe you'll agree with me that some things one just shouldn't hold on to—like gas. That being said, it's always advantageous to be the one who dictates when and where the release of these little "scapeasses" takes place, but alas, as we all know too well, it is not always the way it goes.

I'm hoping that these small tales will entertain and make you feel less embarrassed about the air in your flare. Well, if you are a little shy and inhibited about it, (that'd be normal), let's hope you will be less so once you get to the end of the book.

But not to worry, this little book will just be between you and me and the Queen, as I don't think they'll be making a movie out of it any time soon. It's meant to be a thoughtful gift for that someone special like, you know, for Valentine's Day; for that person who has everything; or for you to read on the throne where you can let 'er rip in all your glory in the privacy of your own bathroom. Yes, it's for just about everyone.

So let's get on with it then, shall we?

So What Is It?

"A chemistry student named Nate
Was heard to remark to his date
Because of the stink,
A fart is, I think,
Poop in its gaseous state."

Flatulence consists of odorless vapors such as *carbon dioxide, oxygen, nitrogen, hydrogen*, a wee bit of the not-so odorless *methane*, and of the most offending fume, *sulfur*.

Like it or not, everyone produces one to four liters of these gases a day, and *everyone* includes you, dear. People will try and tell you that these little "fartlettes" are methane. That's partly true as there is sometimes a bit of methane present. Most vapors passed are odorless. Cows are the valiant champions of methane production, which comes largely from their belching. But they do produce methane from both ends, which is rather extraordinary. So I would suspect methane is not the main culprit for us humans who actually produce a teeny bit of it and only at one end. We'll leave that distinction to cows.

My son, Brandon, says that, on no certain terms, intestinal gas is "the souls of the damned trying to escape." Once they do escape, one might wonder if he's not far from the truth.

Where does it come from?

Some gas comes from the air we swallow when we eat, chew gum, smoke, or have loose dentures. Some of us ingest more air than others when we eat, resulting in more gut reaction, although it is hard to imagine swallowing enough air to cause such impressive activity at the other end.

Other sources of gas come from drinking carbonated sodas and fruit drinks. It seems logical that sodas would produce gas due to the air bubbles, and the fruit drinks would do so as well due to all that sugar, which ferments in our intestines. So barring my philosophy that *all* food is transformed into gas, where else might it come from?

The digestive process alone creates gas. Even more gas is formed if we do not chew our food well enough for it to be digested properly. The stomach gets overloaded and overworked, causing gas production to go into high gear.

Foods produce gas. It would be reassuring to believe that this food, over here, produces gas, whereas that food, over there, does not. But in my experience, *all* food creates gas. According to research though, some foods are worse offenders than others.

Generally, carbohydrates are more gas forming when digested than fats or proteins. Carbohydrates would include foods like whole-wheat flour, flour, cereals, grains (i.e., barley, rye, bran, oats, rice and wheat).

Really healthy foods like the super foods, which include cruciferous vegetables—broccoli, cabbage, sauerkraut, Brussels sprouts and cauliflower—all are gas forming. It doesn't stop there. Other contributors are asparagus, artichokes, carrots, celery, corn, onions, parsley, potatoes, cucumbers, radishes, lettuce, turnips, and rutabagas.

In the category of fruits, many are culprits. This list would include apples, prunes, bananas, dried fruits, apricots, melons, peaches, pears, as well as their juices.

Let's not forget the loved-by-some dairy, cheese, chip dip, ice cream, milk, salad dressings, and eggs.

Legumes, lentils, and beans are exemplary in producing gas attacks.

Not-so-healthy offenders include fried foods, pastries, sweeteners, sugar-free foods, packaged foods, sodas, wine, and beer.

Mother Nature has a great sense of humor, doesn't she? She tempts us to eat all these delicious, natural foods and laughs at us as we fart indiscriminately and uncontrollably in public. So back to my theory that *all* food is gas producing. We are doomed. Now what are you going to eat to avoid gas production? Good luck!

Furthermore, the production of these little stinkers is aggravated by the wrong combination of food in our stomachs.

For example, to reduce gas, eat protein (meats, fish, dairy) with vegetables, and, eat carbohydrates (flour products, noodles, beans, lentils, grains) with vegetables, but don't combine protein and carbohydrates at the same meal. That food combination aggravates the manufacture of the yeasty beasties. That would make a hamburger a no-no, having both protein in the meat and carbs in the bun.

Eat fruit alone.

If you follow these guidelines of food combination, the activity of the fartory will immediately be diminished, giving one a much-needed reprieve but not a total redemption, of course. There has to be some remnants for Mother Nature to laugh at. Sorry.

These food combinations will also cause you to lose weight. Bonus!

What happens when you eat beans and onions? You get tear gas.

Why? Why? Why?

These gas pockets are very functional; although if you or I were in on the designing of the body, we would very likely have circumvented this need. However, Mother Nature, for her amusement, has incorporated the requirement for intestinal gas to help stimulate peristalsis (that's the movement of your intestines to push food down the tube and out) and to herald the load of things to come, sort of like the pipe band that trumpets in the parade.

If the "shitment" isn't dumped when necessary, more and more gas builds up, causing embarrassing situations in the very near future. So that's another source of the problem. If you are a regular fella' or gal, then you would likely have fewer problems in the flatulating department. Keep in mind, whatever your natural endowments are, whether you're a "farteur maximus" or a "farteur minimalus," that having gas is a natural and healthy occurrence.

What is a fart? A turd honking for the right of way.

Why do they smell? The Pewers

These rear tempests can be mostly air and therefore not odoriferously off-putting. Count yourself lucky if you fall into this category. They can be regrettably noisy or, for some unfortunate bloke, both noisy and malodorous. Both scenarios are unwelcomed. If they are just air but noisy, you can cheerfully reassure your company, "Don't worry, its only air!" They'll feel so much more at ease I'm sure (as they roll their eyes). But if yours are pongy, well, that is another story.

Regrettably, some can be quite smelly; we'll call these ones "pewers." So what makes some of these escapees objectionable to your sniffer? Sulfur will do it. The production of sulfur promotes the pungency of these problematic pongy pewers. Yes, the "schtink" comes from bacteria in the large intestine that release sulfur while breaking down undigested food. Smelly methane is also a byproduct of digestion but less so than sulfur.

Some have even suggested we can have a stinky fart gene. There are lots of things in our control, but you have no say in the matter if you are endowed with a stinky fart gene. How bizarre, helpless, and sad is that? So you may unfortunately be the unlucky one who missed out on the big blue eyes and curly eyelashes gene of your brother, but you got the stinky fart gene instead. And you still think Mother Nature doesn't have a sense of humor?

So if your posterior vapors fall into the smelly category for whatever reason, you really are an unfortunate dude, aren't you? What can you do?

Here's a suggestion. If you are the pewee and you have dropped a pewer, make some lame excuse and leave the site immediately so the group left behind will try and determine which one amongst them is the culprit. But if everyone vacates the room due to the offensive fumes, what do you do then? If it sneaked out quietly, don't say anything! Run out of the room with them with an innocent expression on your face, perhaps a bit of puzzlement thrown as if you too don't know what cad could have done such a thing. You'll likely succeed in your ruse.

If the pewers exit quietly, you'll get away with it more easily than your windbag friends whose noisy emissions cannot be concealed. They're the ones who look around for something to blame for the noise—the dog, "Oh Spot, shame on you!"; the cat, "Fluffy!"; the husband, "Honey, excuse yourself"; or in the absence of the above, "Oh this darned chair…"

Farteur Maximus

Doctor: "What seems to be the problem?"

Patient: "Doc, I've got the farts. I mean, I fart all the time."

Doctor nods "mmm"

Patient: " My farts do not smell and they are silent. It's just that I fart all the time. I've been here only ten minutes and I've farted 5 times.

"Mmmm", the doctor mumbles as he takes out his pen and pad and writes out a prescription.

The patient is thrilled. "This prescription, Doc, will really clear up my farts?"

"No", sighs the Doctor. "The prescription is to clear up your sinuses. It stinks like an elephant's arse in here. Next week I want you back for a hearing test."

History of the Fart

Animals and humans roamed the earth for millions of years. They were born. They all farted. They died. This cycle continues to this day.

It's really that simple.

It's a scientific fact that as long as animals are on the earth, they will be farting. Humans fart their whole lives. Some are proud of it; others deny it. But the fact remains; farting is here to stay for all breathing things.

There is a cultural perspective on the fart that has remained consistent throughout the ages. During the course of history, the flatus has been a reliable source of humor. Disgust, yes, but humor too, mainly because it continues to be a social taboo. Why is it that something so natural is so repressed? Because it smells? And people don't like that?

Social veto to express our gas expulsions is, of course, what makes it so funny. Men get away with exploiting this taboo more than do women. They have an ill-gotten sense of feeling manlier after a good toot, but women are not supposed to have gas at all; it's not feminine. When a man passes wind, he farts; when a woman passes wind, she fluffs.

Moreover, when a man farts, the men acknowledge it, and laugh. But when a woman has a "fanny burp," everyone pretends not to have heard it, hoping not to add to an already embarrassing situation.

It also appears to be more acceptable for men to hold and expel as a form of entertainment. I've seen a young man, my thirty-one-year-old son in particular, plop himself down in my company, do the cheek lift, and release a whopper as a conversation starter. I can't see my mother doing this, or myself, although come to think of it, as an icebreaker, it might be worth a try.

Some Farts Have Such Personality; They're Just a Riot

We seem to have a special compartment—a fart-producing chamber if you will, which I'll call the gas factory, or the fartory—in our abdomens. For some, the workings of this part can be very noisy and quite audible. People make unconvincing excuses: "Oh, is that me, or is that you?" "You must be hungry!" "Is that the dog?" Or embarrassed, look in another direction so their eyes fall away from you and pretend they didn't hear anything—it being easier to play deaf than to find an appropriate comment.

I can feel the fartory working overtime, and I know what's coming. The darling "fartlings" hide in my caboose, pushing to get out past that little sphincter that won't let them out until it gets a command from the brain. But they are multiplying at such an alarming rate;

the pressure is on, and often the brain has to relent to the har-ass-ment of the "assgas."

Most of the time, it's simply not appropriate to let them out, even when under the duress of their mighty force. But the little "asscals" have a mind of their own, and they squeeze out or as the sensation goes, fall out through the poe-poe hole. You never know how they're going to pass; you just fear that they may be disobedient to your will and make a break for it at the wrong time and place. And they do. They have no sense of timing or decorum, and they are full of naughty surprises.

Big air pockets from my inner gas factory would sometimes tumble out uncontrollably, one at a time, loud enough that you'd think the noise came from the impact of their hitting the ground. They are hard to ignore when this happens in public, but I try.

For example, I was in the bank the other day, standing at the teller's window. You know how quiet banks can be. I didn't see anyone behind me, so I thought the bank was empty. This observation only mattered because of what my delinquent derriere air was about to do. Totally out of my control and much to my chagrin, a fanny expletive blurted out unexpectedly. And it was not quiet. I'd refer to that "airarsement" as a *braaackkk* type in the flatulus largamus category.

I tried to ignore it so I could pretend to the teller that nothing had happened—nothing that I was aware of at least—but I wasn't sure if someone had come in while I was busy at the counter. So I slowly turned around and sure enough, there was this elderly gentleman sitting on the chair just a few feet away, waiting his turn. Blush. There were no words in the world to get out of this one. I could only really, really hope he was very hard of hearing.

Since I couldn't make myself invisible nor could I hide what had occurred, I displayed the attitude "What was that curious noise?" I looked down and noticed I was fortunately standing on a rubber matt. "Oh, it must have been my shoe on this old rubber mat!" As my foot squirms on the carpet, I look at my foot as if to say, "Bad foot. Be quiet."

Yes, the "brackers" have many personalities, such as in wee air bubbles that come out in groups. This is really engaging. "*Phtt, phtt, phtt, phtt*" like a "rat-a-tat-tat" effect. I picture them bouncing around in there and then escaping through the gate, holding hands and dancing their way out, hitting the air in B flat.

There are the SBD ones (silent but deadly). There is nothing more to say about them. They speak for themselves.

I've talked to my mother about controlling these little assbrats because I've noticed that when I go out in public, such as concerts, movies, and shopping centers, people are very well behaved in this department. I hardly ever hear others making mistakes. So I called on her wisdom to enlighten me how this is so when my own misbehave in such an irreverent manner. After all, she is the expert in this area and my mentor. "Well," she said, "you let them out slowly so they don't make any noise."

Oh really? You let them out slowly, do you? As if I have any control over them. "Wait till we get home." Not going to happen. "Slow, slow, now, easy does it…" They are in such a hurry. They don't listen to the commands of the boss, the brain, and they blurt out—sometimes with impressive acoustics. They are, to put it mildly, irrepressible and uncontrollable, and they don't give a do-rotten-dum-de-dum where I am.

'Roids

Anyone blessed with a case of 'roids (hemorrhoids), or a "ring of fire," understands the complications that they can pose when it comes to the passing of wind. As if the little monstrous gaseous bubbles of air are not unconscionable enough in their own right—loud, rude and objectionable—they resound in full orchestration with the help of 'roids.

My mother advises to release the assbrats slowly so they will come out silently. Silence is in direct contradiction to the effect the 'roids have on assgas. The 'roids tend to flutter and amplify the already embarrassing farting noise rather like the infant who blows air through closed lips to produce the famous, raspberry.

There is no ignoring the magnifying effect of 'roids on escaping flatus. They succeed remarkably in exacerbating already terribly shameful situations.

'Roids also make the passing of the flatulence sound rather, if you'll excuse the expression, wet. This worsens an already humiliating moment because onlookers now believe you've messed your pants.

The Elevator Caper

Flick and Flack had been really good friends when they were growing up, and as luck would have it, after they graduated from university, they worked as engineers in the same building. They habitually met for a drink over lunch. They would go to the bar and have a beer and then down a toasted meat or egg sandwich in the cafeteria—a potent combination for gas production. They were fuelling up for the trip back to the office in the elevator where they held their daily competition. It was a race to release their prize just before getting off the elevator and to convince everyone on board that it was the other guy.

Not only were their rear end obscenities noisy, they were also smelly. The worse that the emissions were, the more important it was to be convincing that it was the other guy who was the offender.

They found the dumbfounded expressions of the victims boyishly hilarious. People are so darned polite. Rather than say anything, they just hold their breath with the result that their eyes get bigger and their faces redder 'til the elevator reaches their floor.

Exit lines for our boys included ones such as these: "That's pretty gross, man," "Take it back," "What would your mother say?" "Aren't you going to excuse yourself?" "No more beer and sandwiches for you," "You didn't…!" "Don't look at me!" "You dirty rat, how could you…?" *Brackkkkk* "On that note…"

The elevator doors would close behind them, leaving the innocent onlookers bathing in their noxious fumes as the engineers guffaw their way back to work like a couple of immature school boys.

What happened to the blind skunk? He fell in love with a fart.

Unexpected company

It was about eleven o'clock at night. Harris had just enjoyed a fabulous meal with friends on the seventh floor of the apartment building, and it was time to head home. So he walked down the hall, pressed the elevator button, and reflected on the evening's discussions.

The elevator door opened, and he stepped in. The gourmet dinner was worming its way down his intestinal tract when he felt a gentle nudge on his lower sphincter, indicating that a biological discharge was required.

With reasonable inhibition, he complied. After all, it was after eleven o'clock at night. Everybody would be in bed or at least at home watching TV in their PJs— not catching the elevator. So in one glorious *blast* of rectal retribution, his gut-wrenching, vile-smelling virus filled the enclosed space with such an overwhelmingly pungent gaseous putrification that even the Grim Reaper would've sought refuge.

Then suddenly, the fifth floor's light blinked on just as he passed the sixth floor. *What? Ooooooohhh my gaaaaawwwwdd!* he wailed to himself. *This can't be happening.* Nowhere to go, nowhere to hide. There was no escape. And worst of all, no one else to blame. He was *so* completely and totally *busted.*

Ping!

The elevator door opened, and an attractive young couple entered in mid-conversation. They were upbeat, lively, and flirtatious. *Oh geez. Why couldn't they have been deaf, dumb, and blind with severe sinus conditions? But no, that would be too easy.* It felt like an eternity—waiting like a stone gargoyle—for his imminent shame to hit their yet innocent and unsuspecting nostrils.

When the inevitable happened, the couple stopped dead in their conversational tracks as the scorching alien fumes seared their nasal cavities. They gagged reflexively, held their breath, and waited desperately for their escape when the elevator would reach the ground floor, which seemed to be taking *forever*. It was suffocatingly claustrophobic. No one spoke. They all knew the score. They were all dying to get out—the couple, for the debilitating stench, him, for the mind-numbing embarrassment.

Ping!

Ground floor. The young couple raced out of the elevator and into the outdoor parking lot, gasping desperately for some fresh air. He dashed in the opposite direction, out the front door, and onto the street, seeking total anonymity and some shred of dignity. Once outside, Harris could hear their shrill voices, laughing and squealing over their shared ordeal.

He could see them through the parking lot fence. They, gratefully, were completely oblivious to him.

"That was disgusting."

"I nearly puked."

"That guy was rotten to the core."

"It's a good thing we didn't get on from the twentieth floor. I would've died of asphyxiation."

"Would you have given the eulogy at my funeral?"

"Written your obit too."

As Harris was listening to the couple's remarks incognito, he was wrestling with two competing emotional responses. One was a crippling, shrinking sensation commonly known as soul-sucking embarrassment. Conversely, the other was an uncontrollable compulsion to burst out laughing while patting himself on the back for a job well done. Strange bedfellows those two.

Harris learned that he would, in the future, simply take the stairs, allowing nature to freely follow its woe-begotten course.

The Fuller Brush Lady

The Fuller Brush lady was pounding the pavement, selling her wares with the pride of a peacock, convinced that her products were absolutely the best the market had to offer. You could see how proud she was in the way she walked, with her shoulders squared and her chin slightly raised as if it were attached with an invisible string to something up in the air.

She was presently working a large apartment complex and had made it to the twelfth floor. Deciding that that was enough for one day, she headed for the elevator. When the doors opened welcomingly, she got in and placed her bags down by her tired feet and pressed the ground floor button. She closed her eyes for a moment of peace and relaxation.

Well, her eyes weren't the only things to relax, and her mouth wasn't the only thing that gave a sigh of relief. *Oops! Uh-oh.* Her fanny sighed in sync, and it was a stinker. She was alone, thank goodness, but she was still sheepish at what she had done. "No matter," she spoke to herself, "I'll fix that up in no time with my pine fresh room spray." And she took out a spray bottle from her arsenal. Phishh. Phishh. "There we go. Fuller Brush pine-scented room spray to the rescue." Feeling very smug, she returned the spray bottle to her bag and resumed her proud posture.

At that moment, the elevator stopped, and in walked a disheveled man, smelling of alcohol. *A drunk*, she surmised. He staggers past her to get the support of the back wall. *Shniff, shniff, shniff.* "What the hell'sh that shmell?"

"What do you smell?" she asks politely, expecting him to comment on the fresh scent of pine from her superior product.

"It shmells like shomwon shit a Chrishmash tree."

The Yoga Position

Lisbeth really wished her toot-chute were quiet. For the most part, her toots were quite melodious—well okay, noisy. They were full of beans—no pun intended. Mischievous. They'd wait for the exactly right, malapropos moment for the bum rush.

For example, she was at yoga class the other day. The teacher had everyone in knot-like positions, and the room was quiet as a Mormon Church. You could have heard a flea fart. Lisbeth contorted her body to agree, sort of, with the instructor's—her bottom up in the air with her knees around her ears with her arms stretched out on the floor along her thighs—when she realized that this position compressed her fartorium, and a feeling of dread came over her.

Ilene Dover

She tried to constrict that necessary little muscle in her butt to stop the gale within, but it was next to impossible in this position; it was as if she were sitting on a toilet upside down. Too late. A big one decided to pop out of her poe-poe hole—yes it did—into the quietness, nice and loud for everyone in the entire room to hear. *Brrussssbbrrrkk*. She stopped breathing for a moment. She wasn't sure what to say. Should she pretend no one heard it? No everyone heard it! Or should she say, "Excuse me"?

Lisbeth didn't want to fess up in the quiet of the room, so she decided not to say anything, reassured with the thought that maybe no one could be absolutely positive from which bottom it ventured.

Lizzy decided then and there that yoga wasn't for her after all, and she never did return to class.

Bowel Boosters and the Big Mistake

Do you remember the days when "they" put locks on public bathroom doors and tried to charge a dime for performing nature's most pressing function? This was common at large gas stations on major highways in the sixties. Fortunately, it didn't last long due to public outcry and likely a few accidents, but I'll always remember the little ditty on one of these bathroom cubicles:

> Yesterday, was broken-hearted,
> Spent a dime, but only farted.
> Today I thought I'd take a chance,
> Saved a dime, but sh__ my pants

Never trust a fart. You never really know. Believing it is just air—and it isn't—can happen at the most inopportune time. Actually, any time it would happen would be inopportune. It could ruin your day. In fact, it most certainly will ruin your day.

It goes somewhat like this. We hope and pray that this next one is just a draft because if we are not in a very quiet place like a church, we may be in a restaurant, looking lovingly into the eyes of our date whom we are trying to impress. You can be sure it'll be in a public place because Mother Nature does have that twisted sense of humor and oops—Bingo—there you have it; you release a quiet runaway, but it isn't just air. You make a beeline to the first washroom you can find to check things out because you are *just not sure.*

One has to be particularly cautious when one takes those little "bowel boosters," which can be either in the shape of innocent-looking little brown pills, or they can come in powder form or as cookies. The preamble that ensues before they take effect could rival the fireworks on the first of July. The feeling is that the gas factory is working overtime and that the little "fartogens" are on steroids as they pop out like jet-propelled missiles, each with their own individual charming sound.

I've come out of the backhouse at the cottage feeling like I've just given birth to ten pounds of air when I thought I was on red alert for action. You truly never really know what the outcome will be. When it comes to your experiences, expect the worst, and be prepared for the worst.

Be warned that these "ass faults" are not to be trusted. Do not make the big mistake of thinking they are just air, especially after taking bowel boosters.

Wanda Releases a Wet One

Wanda worked in a major plaza of a large city. She looked forward to her lunch breaks when she would meet up with her husband, Bob, who also worked in the vicinity.

It just so happened that on this particular day, on her way to the restaurant where she was to meet Bob, she would start feeling the effects of the Russian oil that she had taken the day before to alleviate her ongoing constipation problem.

There was a sense of urgency this time. The pressure was explosive, and Wanda was not confident that the release would be just air. The little "farggers" really wanted out. She furtively looked for the nearest washroom. Unfortunately for Wanda, there was not one in sight. The onrush was irrepressible, and as she feared, the gust that flew from her keister was not just wind.

Horrified, she felt liquid run down her leg under her pants. She backed up against a wall of the wide pedestrian corridor of the shopping complex, praying to be invisible to onlookers or at least hoping not to appear so obviously in peril.

She started walking, clinging her back to the wall, putting one foot beside the other, taking baby steps ever so gently—feet apart, then together, apart, together— until what seemed like forever, she finally came to a women's store. She zipped in the large entranceway, keeping her back from any lingering public. When the saleswoman approached her, she bleated, "That. I'll take that." She pointed to a rack of skirts. "Size 12." She ran to the fitting room, whipped off her trousers, cleaned up as much as is humanly possible, and put on the clean skirt.

Bob, upon seeing her wearing something completely different than when he left her in the morning and noticing her flaming red cheeks asked, "What happened?"

She curtly replied, "Let's just say I have a new respect for Russian oil. How do you like my new skirt?"

Prunes, Curds and Posterior Pongies

Penelope and her husband, Paul, were ravenous after a long day's work but had an hour of driving to get home to a hot meal. Penelope travels with prunes in the glove compartment of her car, and she had a bag of cheese curds left over from lunch.

They enthusiastically feasted on the welcomed snack, but it wasn't long before they both bloated like the Goodyear blimp. They remarked how the reaction was so instantaneous. Undisciplined gas built up in the gas chamber, and they prepared for high winds. They found themselves in a state of emergency for immediate release. Neither was suspecting of how foul smelling the results of such a mixture could be, but they were soon to find out. The fact that they were laughing hysterically did not help in containing the inevitable escape of these rowdy, roisterous riots in their rumps.

The pall of reeking gas filled the vehicle. Paul strained to focus on staying on the road through half-shut eyes.

It was a natural reaction to close the eyes, as if the smell would diminish on doing so, or at least it would hopefully prevent the eyes from burning up. Meanwhile, Penelope was scratching blindly on the door rest to find the down window button but succeeded only in pushing the automatic lock on and off. She had never really had figured out what buttons were which, at least not well enough to do it in the dark while she was choking to death.

They were trapped in the fetid smog of their own pongies. Penelope tried to regain control and find the unlock-the-window button. It was mid-winter, and the outside temperature was twenty degrees below freezing with a wind chill factor of double that with the windows open, but the windows had to come down because they believed they would otherwise asphyxiate.

This was, indeed, the most memorable and paramount experience of posterior pongy pongies that either of them ever had or would ever have again. Suffice it to say that this was the last time that the food combination of prunes and curds were *ever* ingested. Reader, be warned!

"Mom, yer beans are really good, but why do ya' always only use 239?"

"Because if I used one more, they'd be too farty."

Out of the Mouths of Babes

Brandon

I remember the time, many years ago now, when I brought my son, Brandon, then four, with me to the bank. It was the middle of winter, and he was bundled up in his snowsuit. We were in a lineup of about eight people, and I was near the front.

Unfortunately, we had not taken care of business before we left home. Not only was nature calling *now*, but also, Brandon began pounding at his snowsuit in his nether zone. I did not know for certain what the problem was, but I could only imagine that something, at this particular moment, had begun to be somewhat troublesome. As he was hammering away with a straight arm and clenched fist, he was also whining that he had to go to the bathroom. I cajoled him into waiting until I was finished. I thought I had won that one, but I had another think coming.

In the dead silence of the bank atmosphere, there was this thunderous noise of a loud, obnoxious fart. Brandon had made the sound with his mouth and immediately started shouting, "Oh, gross, that stinks" while waving his hand back and forth under his nose.

It was one of those moments I was speechless, except to look helpless and say, "Does anyone know this child?"

Herbie

My grandson Herbie is the cutest dimpled thing you could imagine. He is always making you laugh, and you even have to smile when you say his name. He likes to wave his behind around so everyone can admire it, and sometimes, he proudly presents a nice loud "faht," which sends him into gales of laughter. So that's why I call him a little expert on the subject.

I have to be very careful around this child because "Granny Fanny Gas" is just entertainment to him, and it will not be ignored.

It was a sunny day, just the kind of day to meander down to the ice cream parlor with Grampa and the grandkids.. I had little Herbie by the hand. We were walking on the sidewalk with lots of traffic on the street, enough noise to camouflage a gust from my bottom, yes? No!

There I was in heels, wearing my shocking pink mini dress, with my hair tied up with ribbons. Making an indecent noise at this particular time seemed very inappropriate.

However, I was feeling the pressure building up, and I knew I needed to find just the right moment to release. A big truck was passing us, and I took the opportunity. I was a few seconds off in my timing. But who would notice? Herbie would. He yelled, "Who farted?" I ignored him, stifling a reflex laugh, hoping he didn't know the answer, and trusting no one else did, although it was indisputable that they'd all heard the question.

The Ambush of Monsieur Albert

The definition of an *ambush*: "make a surprise attack from a concealed position"—and indeed, that's exactly what these little bombs did to Monsieur Albert. It was just after dark, and Monsieur Albert was sitting on the side of the five-star-hotel outdoor pool with his feet gently dabbling in the water, minding his own business, enjoying the quiet of the evening. There were a few stragglers scattered about, but for the most part, he was able to be absorbed in the moment with few distractions.

Oh, here it comes. He could feel them going for the exit. It must have been the garlic in the salad. Having had lots of experience in this discipline, he decided, as his eyes rolled up to gaze at the stars, that this one would be slow and silent, as he would release it carefully. Gradually but imperceptivity, he took the classic position, lifting one cheek to give it room to pass. He made the mistake of helping it out by giving it a wee push. *Braaaack*. Uh-oh. It apparently didn't need any assistance.

It was one of those cute little—or should I say *big*—surprises, being good and loud after all. It appeared several escapees had ganged up to produce this embarrassing roar. He hadn't counted on the resonating effect of the side of the pool or on the acoustic effects of the night air. Silence fell as the sparse crowd stopped chatting. Amidst muffled snickers, he made himself as small as possible, arose, and tiptoed back into the hotel, hoping that no one would identify him or realize that that ungodly noise came from his bottom. *Mon dieu!*

On Aging

I'm rich! Silver in the hair, gold in the teeth, crystals in the kidney, sugar in the blood, lead in the butt, iron in the arteries, and an inexhaustible supply of natural gas.

The Flyby

For the uninformed, I'm here to tell you that when you are in an airplane, flying high in the air, the pressure on the inside pressing out is greater than the outside air pressing in. If you thought you had a problem on the ground, you ain't seen nothin' yet.

It's a forgiving fact that airplane engine noise is very loud. People tend to read or sleep, so when you are releasing in your seat, no one realizes it. As long as the "releasees" aren't nasty, you'll likely get away with it. You might get away with it anyway. No one will know it's you, *unless* you are in the aisle with your rear end level with someone's head.

As it happened, I was reaching up into the overhead compartments to find my book. It was in a large bag, and unfortunately for the unsuspecting aisle passenger sitting by me, just the act of lifting something heavy pushed in a downward direction my center of gravity, forcing out any air trapped my fartorium.

A complete and uncontrollable surprise this one was. It made me think of Rocket Richard as it shot out like a puck with a roaring noise that unmistakably came from my fanny. In my mind, I could see it knock this unsuspecting man in the head, striking him off his seat.

Embarrassed doesn't cut it. There was no ignoring it or pretending it was someone else or my misbehaving shoe. I was too humiliated to look, but when I sat down, I could hear the sneering snickers and knew they were laughing at *me*. Waaa! How come my mother never taught me how to control these things?

There was no place to run and hide. If there was any way I could have stuffed myself under the seat like a carry-on, I would have. So there I sat in my seat, frozen with shame and feeling very naked, with my head in my book until the plane landed and everybody got off.

The New Stewardess and Old the Vent

It was Layla's first flight as an airline stewardess—back in the days when they called them stewardesses, not flight attendants. She proudly wore her short blue dress with the scarf around her neck, impeccably ironed. Her makeup was carefully applied for this special day, the inauguration of her new career. Layla had just the right amount of perfume on; it lingered lightly in the air as she slid up and down the aisle. She did look like the picture-perfect airline stewardess.

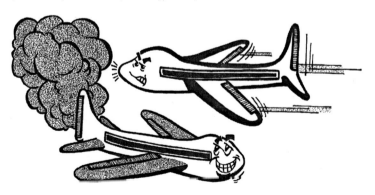

As she was working diligently by herself in the aircraft's kitchen, the galley, she became aware of the most unwanted urge in her fanny. *Oh god*, she thought to herself. *What am I going to do with this? It could be a long flight if I hold on to this the whole time.* She convincingly reasoned with herself, *Well, I guess no one will know since I'm here by myself.* She huddled near the end of the galley, near the unfamiliar vent and got rid of the offending pressure, only to be immediately engulfed in the disgusting stench of her own foul air. *This is really bad*, she thought to herself.

Suddenly the interphone rings. It's the captain. "Oh my gawd, Layla, what the heck did you do in the galley? Did you mess your diaper?"

Layla was so shy and embarrassed about the situation that she quickly explained that it was a passenger in the first row who was the offending party. Apparently, the captain didn't believe her, and he asked her to please come to the cockpit.

She opened the cockpit door to the vision of the captain and copilot, sitting in their seats with full oxygen masks on, the kind with the huge holes for eyes and a big hose coming out of the nose. With a straight face, the captain explained to her that they can smell everything in the galley because of a vent that goes directly from the galley to the cockpit.

The Endearing Fart

The story spread around the company, and Layla's nickname became Farty. Layla learned you can run but you can't hide and no more misbehaving anywhere near that old vent.

F-harts and Relationships

Sparkass and Flatulence had been dating for a few weeks, enjoying the odd dinner and movie. As their interest in each other grew, they wanted to spend more time together, and the issue of releasing gas became more pressing.

As long as they were only together for a few hours, butt-air management was under control. It was when they started staying together for days on end that the problem became systemic. Flatulence was sure her head was getting bigger as she reversed the natural direction of her steroidal gas. It was all she could do to hold it in. The very effort kept her awake at night as she lay in fear of escapees, quietly questioning the unanswerable "Can you fart in your sleep?" As long as she was on guard, she felt more assured. She didn't really want to find out the answer to the question just now.

In the morning, anxious to have some time alone to relax, she would rush to the bathroom while Sparkass was still in bed, hoping he would stay there so she could have some privacy for the intimate moment about to descend upon her. Ah, it felt good to relieve the heaviness therein, but the noise sounded like a thunderstorm at close range. It terrified the spiders and shriveled up the flies. It impressively resounded in the tiled chamber.

When she returned to bed, she was curious if Sparkass heard her deliverance, so she asked him if he had heard any thunder. His negative reply she took as a positive, and it gave her a reprieve. God does have a reason, after all, for guys not paying attention.

It just had to happen, getting caught releasing the first f-f-faht in each other's presence. Flatulence had gone away for a couple of days, and when she got home, Sparkass was so glad to see her, he gave her a big hug, lifting her off her feet at the same time as squeezing her mid-drift. What followed was comparable to the noise of a three-hundred-pound man sitting on a whoopee cushion. It was one of those speechless moments. They couldn't ignore it, so they did what we all would do. Laugh. And they laughed and laughed.

Their relationship had reached a whole new level.

Now it was on to farting competitions: good-morning farts, good-night farts, this-is-what-I-think-about-that farts. No more camouflaging noises in the bathroom by flushing the toilet repeatedly or cushioning the sounds with toilet paper. Pride and a sense of accomplishment replaced disgrace and dismay.

The result of this new lack of decorum led to unabashed farting activity in bed. Flatulence almost blew that sweet dear man right off the mattress, and Sparkass reciprocated by pulling a "dutch oven" on Flatulence— letting one loose and pulling the sheets over her head so she couldn't escape his fusty fumes.

Flatulence fantasized that she'd light Sparkass's gaseous flume one morning when he would least expect it. She'd heard that rump gas was flammable, and she was very curious to put it to the test. She'd be prepared for the morning ritual with a lighter.

He wwing around the room, trying to see his behind, all the time wondering, "What the heck did I eat last night?"

Sparkass indeed!

Bartender Joke

An old married couple no sooner hit the pillows when the old man passes gas and says, "Seven points". His wife rolls over and says, "What in the world is that for?" The old man replied, "It's fart football."

A few minutes later his wife lets one go and says, "Touchdown, tie score…"

After about five minutes the old guy lets another one rip and says "Aha! I'm ahead 14 to 7." Not to be outdone, the wife responds in kind and brags, "Touchdown, tie score."

Five seconds go by and she lets out a little squeaker and says, "Field goal, I lead 17 to 14.

Now the pressure is on for the old man. He refuses to be beaten by a woman, so he strains really hard to produce a goal that would tie up the score. He gives it everything he's got, and accidentally poops the bed. The wife says, "What the hell was that?"

The old man says, "Half time, switch sides."

The Barium Enema

It becomes a necessity at some point in your life to have your pipes checked.

Brace yourself to drink a concoction that tastes like chalk mixed with clay before the X-ray; it is clay actually. You absolutely need to take a laxative to get rid of the stuff or it will stay in you for a month. But don't expect the doctor to tell you this. For some reason, they keep it a secret. Maybe they have the same twisted sense of humor as Mother Nature.

However, I had been forewarned, so I was prepared—I thought.

I won't go into details about the procedure itself. However, the aftermath is particularly pertinent. The laxative was responding well, reassuring me that I wouldn't be clogged up for a month. My abdomen, expanded from the gases building up from digesting this clay, was about to explode. I knew something was up, but I was not prepared for what was to follow.

I was led to a washroom adjacent to the procedure room to rid of the annoying substance. The only other door to the washroom, which was my exit door, was onto a long thin hallway where patients waited in an ongoing line of chairs. I couldn't see what was on the other side of the bathroom door nor did I know it was a waiting area, but the three-inch space at the bottom of the door troubled me. I cogitated, *Why is there so much space at the bottom of the door? Is there anyone out there who can hear me?* All I could do was hope that this was not the case. Certainly, hospital protocol would be more discrete.

The noise that blared out of me was stunning, as in it left me speechless. I even had to ask myself, what was *that?* I tried to control it, but I was in the wrong position to have any say in the matter. I grimaced, put my hand over my eyes, lifted myself up slightly, did the cheek-tightening thing, but to no avail. I gained a new respect for the echoing and amplifying features of a toilet.

Several minutes later, when my performance was done, I gingerly opened the door. I was mortified to see about thirty people (I saw a hundred and thirty at least), sitting outside the door along this hallway, and I was embarrassed that they had been entertained and, at the same time, victimized by the noises of my bottom. I prayed that they hadn't heard it, but I knew better. Why didn't they bottle this stuff for warfare? This was a hospital. I feared I'd be arrested for not respecting the code of silence.

To add insult to injury, I had to walk in front of all these waiters to get to the changing room. My hospital gown was typically done up at the back, where you can see flesh in between the ribbons. They looked at me like you would gawk at a bad driver as you pass him in the passing lane. Humbling!

But the good news is I did live to tell the tale. As embarrassingly horrific as flatulence is, it isn't fatal. Keep it in mind if you go for a barium enema, and don't forget the laxative.

The Proctologist

The dreaded day had arrived. I was off to the proctologist's. If you don't know what this is, just imagine a man in a blue gown putting on a rubber glove and saying, "Bend over." That's him.

I was bracing myself for the humiliating hemorrhoid operation. If I understood it right, he was going to tie an elastic band around my hemorrhoid, and it was going to dry up and fall off. Just thinking of this made me want to be very tiny so no one could see me. How could this degrading situation be any worse? Read on.

The waiting room was dark, the air, stale. It was crowded and full of old people who were supposed to have these problems. They were crammed together single file on school-type wooden chairs, bordering three of four walls with their backs against the wall and their knees lined up in front. Everyone was dressed in grey and looking like they'd just gotten off a refugee boat from "Havenomoneyeevlakia." I may have just imagined it, but I think that they all had scarves on their heads.

I sat there in my white and burgundy pinstriped silk dress with my wide-brimmed burgundy felt hat, and my little heels tucked under the chair, feeling very much like I was in the wrong place.

Eventually, I was ushered into another waiting room. Apparently I was just waiting in a waiting room meant for people to wait until they are put in the real waiting room. I hoped there were only two levels of waiting rooms. This new waiting room had the appearance of the real deal, looking like a lawyer's office with its floor-to-ceiling books and large leather-topped minister's desk. There was even a big dominating portrait of an elderly man in a white lab coat whom I assumed to be the doctor himself. I studied it. He was nicely topped with white hair. *Mmm*, I mused. He has likely had many years of experience at this sort of thing. I thought to myself, *Maybe, just maybe, I could be comfortable with this doctor for this indelicate procedure.*

After an acceptable waiting period, in walks a tall, handsome young man who introduces himself as the doctor. I sputtered, "Aren't you a little young for the job?" *And a little too cute?* I thought to myself. Apparently not.

I was directed into a room that had two doors—not one, but two—each on opposite walls. In the middle of the room was "the table." There was a rectangular block ominously erected in the center, and I was instructed to climb up on the table and put my stomach on the board.

This allowed my bottom to be in the air for the doctor's convenience, but it also had my heels hanging near one end and my head at the other. Keep in mind I still had my hat on. I think this is what you call a Kodak moment.

I was stupefied. There seemed to be about three people in the room, which were way too many for my liking. As the doctor was working away in no man's land, I turned my head to notice that both doors were wide open and people, strange people, were walking around out there. I was sure the doctor was unaware of this insensitive situation, and I immediately sprung up to inform him. This action put pressure on my abdomen—and we all know what lurks in there—and at that totally inappropriate moment, a gaseous expletive shrieked from my behind.

I wanted to crawl under the table and make myself invisible so maybe they would all forget I was ever there. I'm sure the color of my face matched my hat. Deplorably, the situation of the doors didn't change because of my suggestion. They stayed open, and those strange people continued to buzz around.

When all was done, I left with my tail between my legs, so to speak—with the elastic band securely in place.

And that is how a bad situation can get worse.

The University Coed

Bridgette was a gorgeous buxomous blond on her first date with a third-year engineering student. She was in her first year of business and had met Brad the week before in the library. He had taken her to the swank fraternity lounge for a white-tablecloth dinner. Brad's friend Joe, also in engineering, joined them for cocktails.

As the three of them were sitting there in unfamiliar luxury, Bridgette carried the conversation, laughing at the appropriate times and giving a good impression, not just a pretty face.

However, one of her laughs was overly exuberant for her gas chamber, which at that moment, was full. Out popped a winner. She was grateful it was inaudible as that left everyone wondering who did it. Yes, three was the magic number, each looking at the other two and ending up none the wiser. The smell, however, could not be ignored.

The incongruity of the situation was overwhelming. There was nothing Bridgette could do but pretend she was graciously handling someone else's mishap.

She eventually did tell Brad that she was the guilty one that night after they had been married for several years.

The Tootin' Pony, Windy

Windy was a proud member of the riding academy. He was white with black spots, and he had a long, shiny white mane. He was perfect for the beginner rider—tame, friendly, and entertaining.

Kids would gather around the arena just to watch Windy trot around the circle because each time his hooves hit the ground, he would let out a toot. *Toot, toot, toot, toot,* around and around he went.

Students came from other riding schools to see this famous little pony trot and toot around the ring. The young riders would watch and giggle. Everyone loved Windy.

Windy entertained the riders for thirty-five years until he went to pony heaven. He was buried on the farm, the only home he knew. The students stood around his resting place, and each said their good-byes, each placing a small bouquet of wild flowers on the loose earth.

Windy left them with many wonderful memories—the most memorable being his tooting. So you see, tooting isn't always that bad. In Windy's case, it was his claim to fame, although I wouldn't go as far as to say that I could ever see that being a desirable destiny for any of us.

What is the difference between an elephant and a bar?" The bar is a bar room and the elephant is a 'BAROOM!!' "

The Misbehaving Guest

It was to be a normal evening spent with friends over wine and dinner. But things took a turn when I had to excuse myself from the table to answer nature's call—you know, that one with the sense of humor. I wasn't sure if it was a false alarm, but I sure wasn't going to try and find out around the dinner table.

Fortunately for me, the bathroom was on the second floor. But this home didn't have the kindness of carpets to absorb any sounds, no, only hardwood floors that have a great capacity to transmit noise.

I found the bathroom just in time for the bombs to drop. I raced for the toilet paper, hoping to muffle the thunders that were fleeing from my fanny. It was a new roll, naturally—the kind where the squares are attached in a big circle and it's impossible to find where it starts. By the time I was done with it, it looked like a cat on acid had been at it.

These grenades were not only making an uncamouflageable racket but were surprisingly rather stinky. There goes the wallpaper. After finishing my business, I noticed an irritating running water sound coming from the back of the toilet. I knew exactly what that was as I had fixed drips before. I was, after all, a homeowner. I'd take care of this.

I gently lifted the lid off the tank. Somehow, it slipped my grip and went crashing down on the tiles. The noise was a secondary problem; the fact that it broke in two was my primary concern. I stood there in grief just looking at it. What was I going to do *now*?

I adjusted the chains inside the tank, which solved the running water problem. However, the tiny bit of satisfaction I felt did nothing to alleviate the dismay of the broken tank top. I picked up the two pieces and fit them together on the tank as best I could; however, I was unable to do anything with the wallpaper. I, now sufficiently demeaned, returned to the dinner party.

The broken top was eventually replaced, but I never did find out how much, if any, of my calamitous, clamorous experience was shared with the dinner crowd. I was too embarrassed to ask.

The Bunion Op

Who would think that a bunion operation would aggravate or ameliorate (depends how you look at it) the already existing problem of passing wind? No one would. Not until you have the operation and find out for yourself. Another little bombshell Mother Nature has tucked up her sleeve.

You see, the fact that you can't bend your big toe to walk properly causes the body to take on an angled posture, with the upper torso tilting forward. This position is perfect for placing the exit route in a straight line for the pongies in the fartorium, facilitating their escape down the poop chute. At the same time, the forward lean somehow makes controlling that little, necessary, constraining muscle more difficult. It now acts more like an automatic door.

One is hesitant to go out of the house due to the enhanced facility for them to exit due to the body tilt. At home, you can turn up the radio or TV or hide in the bathroom and let them out. But going out in public is another story. One can try coughing at the same time to cover up rude noises and hope it has the desired effect. I fear making unacceptable bottom burps from the gas loitering therein at the most unexpected times in public. The risk was always high; the effort, formidable. But now it's *worse!*

For example, I was invited to a Chamber of Commerce breakfast meeting—you know, the ones at seven thirty in the morning, before you've had your morning constitutional? I had to refuse because I knew the possibilities of being preempted by a fart just as I would be standing up to introduce myself due to this body tilt I had acquired.

I decided to pass on that opportunity, thereby getting one up on our barrel-of-laughs friend, Mother Nature. In the meantime, I hope to rectify—or I should say, fix—the posture problem as my bunion operation heals.

The Opera

The rows of red velvet seats flanked by mahogany arm rests and the breathtakingly beautiful chandelier hovering in the empty space over their heads signaled to him that they had dressed appropriately for the occasion—he in his black suit and tie and his wife in her cherry-red formal gown.

They had never been to the opera before, so this was a new experience for both of them. They weren't sure if this would be to their liking or not, but they were looking forward to the evening and certainly willing to give it the good old college try.

Everything went swimmingly well for the first half hour. They sat there spellbound, absorbing the setting, the music, and the costumes. It was as if they had been transported to another world.

Then they were rudely returned to reality by a strange and nauseating odor emanating from a well-appointed woman sitting beside him. He leaned, at first discretely, toward his wife but then contorted even closer as the smell of the vapors intensified, and he experienced a complete nuclear olfactory meltdown. Trapped, he put his hand over his nose in an effort not to die.

What seemed an eternity later, the intermission came, and they left, convinced it wasn't just enhanced rump gas but more like a ruptured, overly ripe colostomy bag. They had no intention of sticking around to find out.

I wonder if they'd chance another opera any time soon.

The Campfire

Ah, to be out in nature in the fresh air, returning to the fundamentals of survival. Living in a tent that offered a flimsy skin to protect us from the elements, collecting and burning firewood for food, using minimum amounts of insect repellent to avoid being eaten alive by the bugs, and enjoying the camaraderie of close family members—yes, this is the life.

Darkness had descended on the campsite. The fire was burning robustly, and the wieners at the end of the long sticks were sizzling nicely. It was a clear night, and when they weren't looking at the fire, they were gazing at the brilliant stars overhead.

It was about then that my husband leaned over inconspicuously toward my father's, Tabber Knack's, camping chair and in the darkness, started to tickle his bottom by rubbing his fingers lightly on the canvas from behind.

Tabber squirmed a bit, trying to scratch by wiggling in his chair, but it wasn't long before he caught on to the ruse. Wisely, he didn't let on.

He turned to my husband, who was sitting beside him, and asked him to check under his chair to see if there was anything there. My husband, to safeguard his innocence, of course, obliged.

Tabber waited for his head to be under the chair to expel the stored bundle of vile gas accompanied with the appropriate sound effects. My husband roared, "Tabber Knack, what have you done?"

Everyone laughed at him mercilessly. Everyone, that is, but my husband, who had been caught and paid for his misdemeanor with a small amount of humility.

The Endearing Fart

The Old Man in the Nursing Home

The old mvoutside his room on a chair, waiting to be taken down to dinner. He was situated right across from the nursing station, so the nurses could keep an eye on him. They noticed that he was tilting to one side. "Mr. Johnson, be careful you don't fall," they cautioned, as they propped him back up. He tilted again. "Mr. Johnson, be careful you don't fall!" They propped him up again. This happened a few times before they decided to secure him with a sheet by tying him upright to his chair. "We don't want you falling, Mr. Johnson." The next day the inspector dropped in and asked Mr. Johnson how he liked it in the home. He said the food was good, the staff were pleasant, he had no complaints except that it was hard to have a good fart.

The Fan Fart

Lisa had the family over for Thanksgiving weekend. This included Lisa's daughter Marnie and Marnie's boyfriend Royce, Lisa's son and his wife, and their little girl, Cherie who was four.

When it came time to go to bed, Lisa hospitably showed them their beds. Not sure whether her daughter was sleeping with Royce or not, she offered them each a different bedroom.

In the morning, Lisa got up early to make breakfast. The door to Royce's bedroom was opened, and she noticed the bed was still made. *Oh, I guess he's in with Marnie*, she absently observed, and on she went to the kitchen.

She took out the milk and eggs for the pancakes, then the eggs, bacon, and jam. The upright position after a night's rest called to arms the trumpets in the barracks. Confident no one was up, she let 'em out. It was questionable whether or not the sound effects were within earshot of her sleeping guests.

She was soon to find out. Shortly thereafter, Cherie comes into the kitchen, rubbing her sleepy eyes, and says to her gramma, "Gramma, that was a fan fart." Surprised at her arrival and at her comment, Lisa asks, "Why a 'fan fart'?" Cherie explains in her little girl voice, "'cause it was long and fluttery." Lisa's laughter was interrupted only by that of Royce's who was sleeping, after all, on the sofa in the family room off the kitchen.

Well, do you think Lisa ever heard the end of it? Forty plus years later, at family reunions, special occasions, weddings, and funerals, Royce is there to remind her of her unfortunate blunder made many years ago in the kitchen.

What do you call someone who doesn't fart in public?
A private tutor.

The SBD One

I've included this one because I'm pretty sure churchgoing people would never buy my book. I thought this would not be offensive to the non-churchgoers. If you are a churchgoer, my apologies.

When the church organ stopped reverberating in the walls of the church, the minister somberly arose to churn out his sermon. His thick voice droned on in typical fashion—in long drawn-out words and extended pauses—which he used to emphasize his points as he glowered down on his captured audience.

Everyone seemed spellbound, or asleep. In the mesmeric atmosphere of the day's lesson, "Daddy," sitting obediently on the hard bench, released an SBD (silent but deadly) one. When the realization hit him that it was a SBD, he shifted slightly in his seat, looking up at the ceiling, hoping that Jesus would answer his prayer that no one would realize it were he.

There is safety in numbers, to be sure. He was almost convinced his prayers had been heeded when the putrid air hit Lacy's nostrils. Lacy was his four-year-old daughter who, up to this point, was behaving angelically beside him.

The moment of Lacy's awareness coincided regrettably with one of the minister's elaborate pauses. The silent church air was filled with Lacy's squeal, "Oh, Daddy, you really stink!" She plugged her nose in protest.

As the "onhearers," "onsmellers," and onlookers gradually became aware of what "Daddy" had done, the somnolent congregation broke out into a communal belly laugh. Busted! As he sat there entertaining everyone, he asked himself, "Is this hell?"

Confucius was right when he said, "He who fart in church, sit in own pew."

St. Valentine's

The old folks decided to go to the dollar store and buy something for the grandkids for Valentine's Day.

The Valentine section was bursting with red things like hearts, hats, stickers, necklaces, etc., all things to delight a loved one. They needed to find something flat to send in the mail, nothing too big as postage from Florida to Ontario was pricey.

They were looking at the pretty girly things for the granddaughter when he let out a noise that sounded like a water-logged rubber ducky. She couldn't understand the surprised look on his face. His eyes were sort of widening, and his lower jaw hung loose as his eyes darted sideways and upwards. He must have known it was coming, dontcha' think? Alright, maybe it was a surprise attack.

Like a couple of silly kids, they started to quietly laugh; at which point, she replies in resounding harmony. Now they both looked dumbfounded and after a pregnant pause, started to laugh again. Then a little on the late side, they sheepishly looked around to see if anyone was within earshot.

They seemed to have gotten away with it this time. Maybe people would have excused them because of their age anyway.

It's not in every situation that bottoms can sing out loud without inhibition and not be discovered. They were delighted that their fannies got along so well!

They quickly picked up some hearts and stickers and made for the cash before a recurrence could happen. They didn't want to push their luck.

I Hate My Little Brother

Why did God have to invent little brothers? The world was fine without them. My life was fine without one.

Somehow, somewhere, sometime, my little brother, Sid, had surpassed me in size and strength. I barely noticed it until he started winning our wrestling bouts. I was no match for his testosterone. I had to outsmart him now using my brain. This was like taking candy from a baby.

He didn't like my new military tactics, which made him feel intellectually inferior. I had to reassure him, "You *feel* intellectually inferior because you *are* intellectually inferior." This was provoking him beyond his limited capacity for stress and humiliation. I had no idea how far he would go to get even, but I was soon to find out. He had decided to counter-strategize, increasing his forte, his brawn.

One night, he was waiting for me outside the bathroom, waiting for me to finish up, waiting for me to walk unsuspectingly out of the bathroom toward my bedroom. It was a well-crafted surprise attack against the unprepared enemy.

I absentmindedly turned off the bathroom light and turned around the corner to the hall. It was at this moment that I tripped on his extended foot and fell to the floor. In a millisecond, he was on top of me with a wicked plan to subjugate his foe. What he did next made me really hate him. I didn't speak to him for months, not more than one-word answers unless I absolutely had to.

The brat sat on my face and let loose gas that had been saved for days—putrid, foul gas that sprayed all over my face. Since he was sitting on my head, I couldn't escape until he decided to free me. Long moments passed with my useless screeching pleas for reinforcements echoing through the empty house. "Anybody out there? Will somebody please *help me*!"

What seemed like forever, he got up and gloated his victory over my wretched, defeated soul.

I hate my little brother!

Fresh Air in the Hills

The ladies' delightful little fannies were well defined in their tight-fitting ski suits. It was quite a sight to behold in the lineup for the slalom race at the base of the ski hill. So many brightly colored ski outfits dotting the white snow, all filled with enticing curves. The guys were not oblivious to the eye candy.

The people in this crowd of good-looking skiers were all body-beautifuls. They had the hair. They had the teeth. They had the form. They had the looks. And seemingly, they were athletic and good skiers too, being there, part of the race.

The fresh air gave them that ruddy, healthy look; the puffs of frosted air coming from their mouths and nostrils only enhanced an already impressive image. This is how the other half live—affording the sport and having the wherewithal to pay for all the trimmings: the outfits, the ski passes, the meals, the nightlife, and the chalets that went with it.

It was most incongruous and unfortunate that one of the adorable little bottoms in that crowd, at the foot of the hill, on this particular day, at this specific race, at this exact moment, there in the fresh cold air, leaked a mushroom of hot air, which was only slightly visible to anyone who may have been gazing—ogling?—in that direction. Wretchedly for her, it may have been a few, quite a few.

So anonymity was not an option. It took a mere few seconds for the impact of her treasure to take effect. Whew! It was a choker. The skiers gradually went into reverse in formation to find some fresh air as imperceptibly as possible. They were talking through their noses (because they were, at the same time, holding their breath), trying to divert attention from the cutie, who must most certainly be mortified.

As names were called for the race, they reluctantly returned to the lineup, only to be greeted by the lingering residue of her offering. They had to stand there in the foul air, befuddled that a little breeze didn't come along to dissipate it.

There are some things even money can't fix!

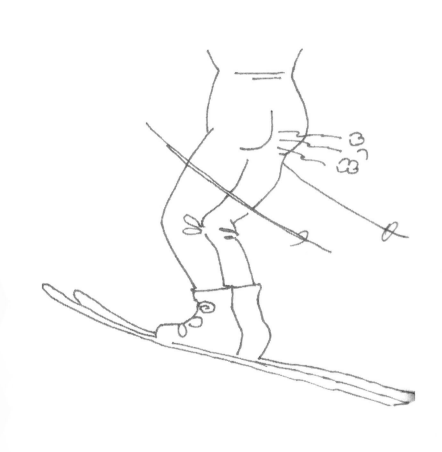

Massage Therapy

Bruce and his lady, Barbara, had decided to treat themselves to a massage to celebrate their third anniversary. They headed down to a recommended spa, which they had not yet had the opportunity to visit. However, the appointments were made, and they went with the assurance of a good referral from a reliable friend.

Their first impression is that it was bright and clean, very spa like, certainly up to their expectations. The atmosphere instilled confidence that this would be an enjoyable experience.

After a reasonable time passed, an elderly gentleman entered the room and ushered Barbara away for her massage. *Mmmm*, concluded Bruce, *I guess a bunch of old fogies work here. Ah, well, I'm sure they know their trade.*

Totally anticipating an elderly man, Bruce just about fell off his chair when a beautiful, tall, bosomy blond came in next and invited him to follow her. Of course, she had on a mini skirt, which showed her long, lanky legs, and a low-cut top that revealed, you guessed it, lots of cleavage. "Y-y-yes, I'll f-follow you, w-with pl-pleasure," he drooled to himself silently. *This must be the secretary,* was the thought racing through his mind.

She led him to a room with a massage table and invited him to prepare for the massage. He could remove his shorts or leave them on, whichever was more comfortable. At this point, he was thinking, *Omg, I think she* is *the massage therapist.*

She discretely left him to his own devices. He quickly stripped, lay on the bed, and pulled the cool sheet up over his naked body. *This just doesn't seem right*, he reasoned with himself. *I feel like I'm cheating on Barbara.* He jumped off the massage table and quickly put his shorts back on and darted back under the sheet, feeling just marginally more comfortable.

The masseuse came in, and yes, it was she. He tried to relax as her hands spread lightly scented oil all over his back. As she leaned over his head to stretch her arms down to his waist, her breasts rubbed against his head. *Holy cow! I hope my little man behaves himself. Down boy!*

As this thought raced through his mind, she was pressing down firmly on his lower back. It was as if she had flicked a switch from Hold to Release, and out of his butt rumbled a big fat cloud of pongy fumes. *Oh no*, he moaned to himself. *Thees ees not poseeeble!* He sputtered a pathetic apology. She quickly made some excuse to leave the room.

After the massage, he and Barbara headed home. He felt it better not to share the details of this little excursion, preferring instead that Barbara rest with the assumption that his masseur was an old fogy too. Besides, he was too embarrassed to speak.

The "Oh No, No, Not Now!" Fart

The newlyweds arrived at their honeymoon haven on a quiet island in Hawaii. They were understandably stressed out from the wedding and were very ready for a relaxing time together. Is there a limit to relaxing? Well, let's see.

It was stereotypically romantic: the palm trees swaying in the tropical breeze; the setting sun, red of course; the beach, stretching for miles; and the hotel band trio singling liltingly in the background.

In this surreal setting, they dined, they danced, and they went to bed. Ah, the nuptial night at last. This would be the first time they'd be together as man and wife, a very special moment indeed. But unfortunately, they had not put into the equation that all that Hawaiian food took time to digest, and that time was right about now.

They were cozying up on the king-sized bed with its overstuffed pillows and crisp cotton sheets. Then it started. She could feel it. The gas factory was kicking into overdrive. "Oh gawd," she begged some unseen power, "not now!" But it was too late as she was already feeling the weight of his body bear down on the gas warehouse in her belly. Before she had time to jolt out of her unwound, relaxed state and engage the guard, the deplorable gaseous shooters thundered from her behind. *Bbbrrraaaack!* they roared as they ripped past the gate.

She was fartagusted. He was fartaghasted. They lay there in suspended silence, frozen as they assessed the situation, trying to find some appropriate thing to say, and hoping to do so in a matter of a few nanoseconds. His towel rack immediately went south as he gawked at his beloved, his lil' cootie-patoody, who was gawking back at him with eyes wide and bottom lip stretched under her lower teeth, an expression acknowledging her certain guilt. They simultaneously decided the best thing to do was laugh, but the magic of the moment was gone.

They turned on the TV, wondering what to do for an encore or at least wondering what would be next. Married life certainly had started off with a bang, so to speak.

NASCAR Nerds

NASCAR races attract all those devoted NASCAR fans to a place where they can all marinate in their shared bravado, in their dedication to the sport, and in their blossoming group intelligence. It's an inspiration, really.

This time they were in Michigan. The Canadians had installed themselves nicely in their camp with their truckload of Molson and Labatt 50. They didn't need much else to sustain them over the weekend except some caloric intake like heart clogging nonfood items and the traditional hamburgers and steaks.

It wasn't long before the Americans in the next camp had sniffed out the sought-after Canadian beer. Where there's a Canadian, there's Canadian beer, eh? A gang of four bare-chested hunks came over to suck up for a hand out. Well, the Canadians weren't pushovers, you know. These guys had to work for it like trick or treat, mature, adult style.

The Americans were prepared for the challenge. They were apparently really talented. Two of them could sing "The Star Spangled Banner" all the way through. Average, one might quickly conclude. But these were not your normal American boys. These ones were exceptional. They were able to sing "The Star Spangled Banner" through their butt cheeks, or so they claimed.

This would be worth a few Canadian beers for sure. Our Canadian guys got the expressions set on their faces—lips closed but smirking, conveying they didn't believe it for a minute. I mean one has to admit, that is a lot of gas one has to store to be able to "sing" a full song, especially a long one like "The Star Spangled Banner."

The Americans postured themselves for the performance. This alone earned a few pints. The one wearing a Speedo positioned himself on the floor on all fours, while another guy sat backward on him, saddle style. Perched this way on his back, he could tap his butt. And off they went, in sync, the one on the floor releasing a spurt of gas each time the one on top tapped his cheeks, not missing a beat for the entire song.

Truth be told, they unbelievably did not only one but two songs.

The Canadians were laughing so hard, they were regretting downing so many beers beforehand as they were uncontrollably wetting their pants.

The Americans deserved a *lot* of beer for this one. This story would go down in the anals, or rather, annals of NASCAR history.

Giving Blood

Astie hated needles. She knew that but decided to give blood anyway. This turned out to be a bad decision.

In retrospect, she surmised that she had gotten caught up in the crowd phenomenon of following the group. That day, if the fifteen coworkers had decided to go for pizza, she likely would have gone too. If they had decided to go to Happy Hour, she's pretty sure she would have tagged along. Unfortunately for her, this day, they all decided to give blood.

Reluctantly, Astie went with them. She was only twenty-one. It was her first job, and her first—and last— time to give blood. She didn't like anything about this experience: the setting, the needles, the bags of blood, the cots, and the Band-Aids. Nothing. Not even the donuts.

As soon as the needle went into her arm, she fainted.

When Astie came to her senses and saw the needle in her arm and the bag filling with blood, she threw up.

By now, she had the full attention of her co-workers and of all the other blood donors in the hall. When all eyes were upon her, in the stillness that only a celebrity could command, she farted a booming, flamboyant, brash little horror that engulfed her in a cloud of dark dishonor and disgrace.

She closed her eyes and activated the death wish. "Maybe they won't see me if I can't see them." The disappearing act? Mmm. Where is David Copperfield when you need him? She was royally stuck in the most embarrassing moment of her life.

To her utmost degradation, Astie remained under the curious gaze of the spectators while she cleaned up, picked up her purse, and departed the scene, all the while feeling them tsking after her. She was certain she could hear them calling at her "Asti, you stink! Asti!" She had to return to work with her coworkers. The grueling, gnawing feeling of raw humiliation in her gut did not leave her for days.

To this day, fifty years later, Astie has never again given blood. And of course, her co-workers never let her forget her mishap, which amused them for many years afterward.

Timing Is Everything

It was the kumquat festival in the quaint town of Dade, Florida. What's a kumquat? It's a fruit that looks like a little tiny orange and tastes like one too. It deserved a festival in this little town. There was the works, the parade, the music, and the queen. It was delightful.

The two couples had arrived in the morning and were taking in the sights together. Shortly after lunch, the wives decided to explore the local shops, leaving the guys, Joe and Blake, behind in a small ice cream shop by the courthouse. The duo sat there enjoying the ice cream, watching the people going by, and taking in all of the antique cars on the road that day.

Being guys, they talked about guy things and behaved more like bears than they would with the women around. They're a tad more relaxed. As they sat there, one of the guys, Bob, did the proverbial cheek lift to let the honker out. His friend, Blake, wasn't terribly shocked, just amused—sort of a guy thing to do. What wasn't so normal and what caught them both by surprise was what happened simultaneously to the release of the whoofer.

Exactly the moment Bob so proudly liberated his prize, the clock on the tower of the courthouse gonged one o'clock. *Gonnggg!* It echoed through the square.

The timing was just too much of a co-inkydink. Blake howled, "You hit it!"

They were duly impressed, as they had seemingly just heard the most melodic fart ever. Either that or Bob had particularly good aim.

The Young Executive

A young executive had the honor of being appointed the position of working with a Japanese firm in planning the next big project for his company. He was to meet them for dinner at the company's annual convention, which was being held over the weekend at a five-star hotel. This was an opportunity to represent his company in the most favorable way. After all, he was the upcoming star of the firm.

As his luck would have it, he'd passed a poor night with stomach pains and gas issues from the large corporate dinner he'd had the evening before and was in poor shape to do this ambassador thing. He awoke around seven a.m. and couldn't get back to sleep. He thought the revolt down below might be quieted with a light breakfast. He dragged his sorry ass out of bed and got dressed and headed out. He guesstimated that he could contain his impulse to let a ripper go at least until he got in the elevator.

As he was locking his door, the rumbling in his stomach made him realize that irritating bodily function was a millisecond away. The cheek clench didn't work. To his dismay, he had no more say in the control of this airarsement. The smelliest and in all probability, the loudest fart known to man bolted without restraint from his behind. He wondered if he had indeed crapped his pants.

At that exact moment, the contingent of Japanese representatives turned the corner at the end of the hall, caught sight of him, and waved good morning. Argh! Hoping they had not *heard* him, he meandered down the hall to meet them, believing he'd left the obnoxious stench behind. But to his chagrin, it followed him as if it were attached to his pants. It just wouldn't leave. He walked faster, turned his head to check and it was still there. *Man, what is this? Go away! Get lost!* He made a weak attempt to fan his fanny area as imperceptibly as possible, but the stink stuck in spite of his efforts.

He greeted them in a louder-than-normal voice, thinking that it might momentarily overtake their other senses and camouflage the revolting odor.

He had no idea what they observed. He just kept talking loudly as they piled into the elevator and on to breakfast. Maybe they thought Caucasians had a weird body odor. Who knows?

What he did know was that you only have one chance to make a first impression, and he knew he had blown it.

Granny and Grampa

Granny and Grampa were down in Florida where they spent their winters, away from the cold, cold north. They had a neat little trailer home bunched up with other trailer homes of many other grandparents who were doing the same thing.

Let it be acknowledged that when a person gets to be over sixty-five, those in the younger age group considers them old. This is a little insulting once you yourself become over sixty-five, but that being said, there are advantages to being old. There are many behaviors you can get away with, such as forgetting things and farting.

So that is why what happened to Granny is acceptable if not expected. The only other time it would be amusing would be if it happened to a three-year-old and that three-year-old would have to belong to you.

Granny and Grampa were having their breakfast in the intimate, tiny kitchen in their trailer home. They still had their housecoats and slippers on. Granny realized there is no more sugar for her coffee, so she decided to scoot over to Helen's, two doors down, to borrow some.

As she was puddling along, she decided she would take advantage of this time by herself to get rid of some of those demons lying in wait in her fartorium. She dropped one. *Not so bad*, she mulled to herself, *not too noisy*. Again. *Oh!* And again. She didn't know she had so much gas stored up, but it sure felt good to get rid of it.

Wait. "What's that awful smell?" she talked to herself. Old people do that. "It smells like shit." Old people don't usually use that word, but it smelled exactly like that, and she called it the way it was. Annoyed, she thought, *Has someone not picked up after their dog?* But Granny couldn't see any remnants of a doggy doo-doo. It was the most curious thing.

Then she realized that with each of her toots, a little bit of poop would fall down by her feet. So as she was walking along, it'd be "toot, plop, toot, plop."

Relieved that there were no witnesses, she quickly got the sugar from Helen (she didn't forget that) and hurried home to tell Grampa of her faux pas (she didn't forget that either). No she didn't forget that, not for a long time.

Not So Dumb

We can all be pretty judgmental about others at times. This is especially so when it comes to those who are intellectually challenged. We forget there is such a thing as an idiot savant and probably varying degrees therein. And when we think we have the upper hand, well maybe—just maybe—we don't.

A nurse had a job working in a hospital for mentally challenged children and young adults. She was pretty accustomed to dealing with them, knowing their abilities and limitations and what they could and could not do.

One day, she was sitting with a group of them at lunch. She serendipitously dropped a loud, not-to-be-ignored whopper. She ignored it, of course, thinking she could just convince them they were mistaken if they'd heard it.

"Miss, you farted!" one of them noted. "No, I didn't!" she protested. "Yes, you did!"

"No, I didn't!" she persisted. "Yes, you did!"

"No, no, of course I didn't."

"Yes, you did. We heard you. You farted!"

It wasn't clear if she convinced them of her innocence. She was suspicious enough that she remained slightly humiliated. They had raised the bar on how much she could put over on them. She avoided challenging their perceptions in the future and made an extra effort to hang on to her derriere air whenever they were within earshot.

Billy aged 8, "A whale breaths out of an asshole on top of its head."

The Crinoid

If you think you are having a bad day, consider the sea creature, the crinoid, and just be grateful that you don't share his anatomical curse. This is an organism that has several arms and a very short gut. It attaches to a surface until adulthood, when it no longer needs to be affixed to something and becomes a free agent. If you saw a picture of it, you might even think it was nice to look at. You have probably met girls or guys that were a pleasure to behold. God forbid you ever meet someone with the characteristics of a crinoid.

It's questionable how they even mate successfully. They have the most bizarre physical attribute that exists in the animal kingdom. They are the living incarnation of proof that Mother Nature does indeed have a sense of humor. As mentioned before, these things have a short gut. It starts at the mouth. Now one would think there would be many places the other end of the gut could be. Well, these poor beings have their anus located right beside their mouth.

Since we all evolved from sea creatures, we can only be thankful that this genetic pattern did not survive up the evolutionary scale. Can you imagine what that would be like? If you liked someone, you could give them a kiss; or if not, well, you got it.

So now your day doesn't seem so bad, does it?

Monkey Business

The tour guide and the group of twenty or so tourists had arrived at the Bali Holy Monkey Forest in Bali. They started walking through the jungle, which was teeming with little monkeys chattering and swinging overhead.

Hubby asked the wife if she had any more film. She obligingly said yes, she thinks so. They stopped in front of some ruins, which appeared to be a shrine of some sort. There was a stone pillar topped with a cement lion on each side of the steps.

Wifey put her purse down to get the film out, and with lightening speed, a little monkey put his hand in her purse and whipped out a super tampon. Not only was this very embarrassing, but it was a prized item, which could only be bought in Canada, not in Taiwan where they were presently living.

They and the tourists watched this little imp sit atop the lion's head and peel the tampon like a banana. He was stuffing it in his mouth just as another tour bus arrived. Everyone got out and started to watch whatever the monkey was doing, pointing and laughing and getting quite a charge out of the scene.

The monkey wasn't going anywhere; he had their undivided attention.

The tour guide asked what the monkey had in his little hands and what he was putting in his mouth. Wifey thought to herself, *Okay, who's gonna' explain this to him?* As the hubby and the wifey haltingly tried to answer the guide's question, the color of the guide's face turned from an olive tone to a white pallor. He stuttered that for religious reasons, she was not allowed in the Holy Forest. They had to leave immediately.

One last look at the monkey, who with perfect timing and as if he understood the complicated implications of the situation, turned around so his butt was facing the crowd and in the universal language of passing gas, let out a nice loud fart.

And that was the opinion of this little monkey.

Beans and Buzzards

It was the occasion of the Blessing of the Bikes that explained the hundreds and hundreds of motorcycles that lined the airport tarmac in Baldwin, Michigan, that weekend. A minister would actually broadcast a blessing to the bikes from a large bandstand, go around in a golf cart, and then continue to bless individual bikes. This was a true Bike Mecca.

The boys decided to fit it into their annual motorcycle trip. The six of them rented a little cabin in the woods that only had gas lights for light and an outhouse for the bathroom. For meals, they would jump on their bikes and head for the nearest town for a full plate of bacon and eggs for breakfast or a man-sized meal for dinner, or they would eat on the road. They didn't do much cooking.

After attending the Blessing of the Bikes ceremony, they had worked up quite an appetite. They decided to head for Taco Bells where there was a special on Bean Burrito Supreme. Most of them could only handle one burrito, but not Cawlis. No, he was ravenous and downed two huge servings before they could even hit his stomach to signal he was full.

With their appetites satisfied, they jumped on their bikes to take a quick tour of the area before heading back to the cabin. Not an hour went by when Cawlis felt his fartorium filling up rapidly. "I have to head back *now*!" he yelled urgently over the roar of the bikes.

He wasn't kidding. As soon as they got to the cabin, Cawlis was off his bike, making a beeline to the back house, ripping off his leathers as he ran.

The boys parked their bikes and leisurely made their way to the fire pit where they were sitting in a circle when Cawlis returned from his task. He plunked himself down in the remaining chair, simultaneously ridding himself of some remnant gas from his fartory. The despicable, reeking odor prompted the guys to move away to the other side of the circle while complaining. "Ah, Cawlis, did you die or something?"

The answer to the question came in the form of a large shadow that was cast over the group from above. It was a huge, hungry turkey buzzard, which apparently was of the same opinion. It landed precariously on an overhanging branch and glared ravenously at Cawlis with its black beady eyes.

The gang cried, "Cawlis, move or something! He thinks you're dead! Show him you're not dead!" Cawlis jumps up and waves his arms, and the vulture does indeed fly away.

Forever and a day, whenever a turkey buzzard would be sighted on a ride, the boys would yell at Cawlis to hide. After all, he had proven to be an attractive-looking meal to these birds, and the gang was not going to let him forget it. Nope. Rather, they'd rub it in at any opportunity and refresh his memory of that day the buzzard almost had him for lunch.

Be Prepared What to Say

These indiscriminate and impetuous afterburner wretches do bolt at the most inappropriate times. It's to your advantage to be prepared to alleviate the embarrassing situation by having some witty quips up your sleeve, such as, "It's my mating call." When I said this in the presence of my kids years after my divorce, they'd jeer, "That'd explain why you're still single."

Here are more examples:

◊ "It's only air." (This excuse causes the eye-roll reaction).

◊ The trite "Oh! I must have stepped on a frog!"

◊ How about "Some things one just shouldn't hold on to."

◊ "If you can't fart in front of your friends, whom can you fart in front of?"

◊ "It's my mating call"

◊   "If they're not paying rent, they have to get out."

◊   "My horn works, how about my lights?"

◊   "Excuse me, it's a fax coming through."

◊   "It's the souls of the damned trying to escape."

◊   Or "It's my theme song. Leave me alone!"

◊   Try "What do *you* have to say about that?" and hope they respond in kind.

◊   "Someone in there's saying they love you, buddy."

◊   "It's my favorite indoor sport."

◊   "Ah, toothless wonder! You still don't make any sense."

◊   "Get back in there until I tell you you can come out."

◊   And the all time favorite, "Sad be the ass that can't rejoice." Concluded with, "Mine's pretty happy. How about yours?"

◊   Sometimes, you have to fess up and succumb to the humble "Oh, excuse me!"

Remedies

There are some effective actions we can take to diminish the abominable abdominal activity and its accompanying sound effects.

◊   Digestive enzymes can be bought in the health food section of food stores. They help in the digestion of food, thereby reducing the amount of gas produced in the digestive process. Take them when you eat.

◊   Over the counter remedies for gas.

◊   A daily multivitamin will help the digestive process.

◊   Try probiotics. These are natural microorganisms that help with digestion. Our bodies produce fewer probiotics as we age, causing an increase in gas formation.

◊   Reduce swallowed air by eating more slowly and chewing until the food in your mouth is liquefied.

◊   Reduce the amount of carbohydrates in your diet: eat less bread and fewer flour products.

◊   Be regular and evacuate daily. If you need help, eat All-Bran, prunes, or Metamucil every morning.

◊   Avoid cruciferous foods when going out in public.

◊   Try this herbal remedy: Mix one tablespoon each of anise, fennel, caraway, and dill. Chew a pinch a few times a day.

Poems

Ilene Dover

The Gentleman

There once was a man named Jake
No public scene would he make.
Shy and discrete,
One day he would meet,
A gal named Beverly Lake.

He didn't know,
That the girl in tow,
Although beauty around her abounded,
She was an up-starter,
A rather good farter,
Was proud, held her ground, it was so.

In pubic, he feared,
Her fumes would be reared
In places not terribly suitable.
No matter his pleas,
She released as she pleased,
Leaving Jake embarrassed and miserable.

Make no mistake,
Our good man Jake,
Was made to be cool as can be.
He learned, with speed,
Her noises, to heed,
With a polite, "Do excuse *me!*"

The Rogue

A man tall and fine,
Rich and 'divine',
Just ask him, he'd say so himself.
The women he dated
Were women he rated
According to looks, health and wealth.

Of himself he thought rather highly,
That would be putting it mildly.
So his women would be,
From what he could see,
Only the best in society.

Was he surprised,
When this night he surmised,
Would be the night of his dreams.
He took off her garter,
Well, she was a farter.
Not his type, after all, now it seems.

The smell was so high,
That the end was due nigh,
He couldn't take any more.
He gathered his things,
Put on his wings
And gracefully flew out the door.

Ilene Dover

Little Miss Manny Manners

Cute little Miss Manny Manners
Was as polite as polite could be,
Now dressed so prim and proper,
A lady, for sure, to a 'T'.

Who would suspect for a moment,
That she, in her high heels and hat,
Could make noises fit for a monkey,
A fahter, alas, think of that!

She of course professed not to hear it.
What a lady then could she be?
One just had to guess then, who was it?
Was she the fahter, the fahtee?

None could accuse Manny Manners,
Looking so fine and so proud,
Cause ladies don't faht-if they do so;
They do so, quiet, not loud.

Her cheeks became red; she was blushing.
How guilty she looked, one might say.
The fan hid her face, 'twas such a disgrace,
She hastened to vanish away.

The Endearing Fart

Her perfume dissolved in the odor
As she ran for the door all a-glow.
Say good-bye to her former position,
She's now one of the guys, you must know.

Such is the fate of a fahter,
Be she fine, or lesser than that.
It equals us all, be we short or tall,
Be we but skinny or fat.

Herbie Cuts the Cheese

Herbie is a good boy,
Herbie is a tease.
Herbie is so happy
When he cuts the cheese.

Herbie's good at farting,
He's good at cutting cheese.
Herbie clears the room out,
In farting times like these.

Herbie farts at Bella,
At Cole and Mimi, too.
Herbie finds it funny,
He'd do it to you, too!

Herbie puts his fanny
In the air so high,
Herbie then releases,
At will, what a guy!

Herbie farts and chuckles,
We have to go along.
Let's all join with Herbie
Let's sing with him his song!

Ilene Dover

Mother

My Mother's the Queen of all farters,
To the chagrin of all of her partners.
You think she'd be done,
Having all of this 'fun'
But, no, no, they serve as mere starters.

Hers, mostly raucous and smelly,
One after the other, a dilly.
They can't be ignored,
Most people are floored,
But they don't blame her, they blame Billy.

Bill, a lady he thought he had wed,
But learned she's a wafter instead,
He did take the vow,
He got him a frau,
He now wished he had lost her to Ted.

One'd think she'd be done with her farting,
Some dignity she could be guarding.
"We give up, you've won!"
But she says, "I'm not done!"
Well then, we say, "We'll be parting!"

The Endearing Fart

The casket in the aisle rode so smoothly,
A dreamy, quiet sight to behold.
I'm willing to bet
There's gas in 'er yet,
That part of the story's untold.

Ilene Dover

Which-a-ma-callit?

Fartlettes, fartlings, pongies and honkers,
They have so many names, makes you go bonkers.

Rear tempests, butt bubbles, bottom burps all aside,
Why does it smell like a little rat died?

Barkers or bleaters, hot air, fanny fluff,
Who let it loose? I say, "That's enough!"

Vapors, poe-poe wind, whiffers and cheese,
Enough, already! I plead, "Pretty please!"

Whoopsies or wafters, noise from your keista'
You can leave now, that'd be nice-a-ya'.

Rump din, pewers, or fanny expletives,
Look carefully, now, you'll see where the door is.

The term, 'Baby Boomer' takes on a new meaning,
When did you say that you would be leaving?

Missiles, bullets or machine gun fire,
Don't deny it, it's you! Need I enquire?

Thunders, afterburners, kidding aside,
Don't you have someplace else you can hide?

Air or gas or a keister feaster,
You have to go now; don't wait 'till Easter!

Bursts or blasts or 'shooting the breeze',
This is the moment for you to leave, please!

The Nature of the Beast

Although we act with decorum,
Pretend to be Princesses and Kings,
Some things we can't hide,
'Cause they brew inside,
They come out with noise, nasty things.

We never can tell their arrival,
Be they miasmic or sweet.
But we can surmise,
They are full of surprise,
'Ere in public or private they squeak.

They have no respect for a lady,
A matron, a tailor, a Sir.
It's no good pretending,
And manners be tending,
A malaise for which there's no cure.

Try as you might to repress it,
Matters not be ye old or young.
It's a fault we all share,
Let 'er rip, if you dare,
Your very own song will be sung!

The Endearing Fart

The endearing fart,
From our butt does it dart,
Without it we'd all suffer inside.
So, let it be,
Release it with glee.
It's not comfy or easy to hide.

The social norm
Would have us conform
To withholding our gas for decorum.
I'll not be a martyr,
But rather, a farter.
I'll risk being thought of a moron.

Whether I'm in my bed
Or outside instead,
I'll release my bottomy gas.
To withhold is a sin,
For the pain within,
To that, I'll give it a pass.

Ilene Dover

Though noisy, but free,
Come fart with me,
We'll not be shy or unyielding.
A smelly toot?
Who gives a hoot?
It's a natural, healthy, good feeling.

We all have in common
This shameful phenomenon
Oh dear, what shall we do?
Don't ask your mother,
Your sister or brother.
Let's all toot together, "Yahoo!"

Conclusions

Hail the fart. Whenever. Wherever. Whoever. Its existence actually enriches our lives because it gives us those unforgettable moments that we can recall again and again and again. Yes, those occasions which are always good for squeezing out yet another laugh.

By now, the reader has surmised that he or she has lots of company when it comes to passing wind. The only thing you can do is laugh at it because everyone has it and everyone has to deal with it. You are not alone.

Just a word of advice in closing, if you're taking care of business in the privacy of your own home and the dog next door starts to bark, I would suggest you close the door.

CPSIA information can be obtained at www.ICGtesting.com
Printed in the USA
LVOW09s1103150215

427113LV00015B/374/P

9 781632 680266